MW01291449

QUIET THE MIND

An all-age, art-therapy activity book
to encourage finding peace first from within.

Dedicated to those who dare to dream
with an open heart and open mind.

© **2012-14**
Lynnette Rozine Prock
www.MyDreamsMatter.com

THIRD EDITION

ISBN-13: 978-1479104833
ISBN-10: 1479104833

Self-published thru CreateSpace.com
by Lynnette Rozine Prock

Creacious, INC.
www.creacious.com
Los Angeles, California

In order to **quiet the mind** and direct focus toward your own personal power, simply answer the following lighthearted questions.

Use the next couple of pages to explain in **vivid detail** the most attractive scenario you can imagine.

Color the patterns provided throughout the book if you need help finding stillness. Doodle and sketch.

What's your **favorite color**? Write what you see.

Where is your **dream vacation** destination?

What **foods** or **restaurants** do you love most?

Is there one type of **exercise** that you prefer?

What are your **hobbies**?

Fill the page with this sentence:
I am always present and in the moment.

_____

_____

_____

_____

_____

_____

_____

_____

_____

_____

Fill the page with this sentence:
I manifest abundance by being grateful
for what I already have.

_____

_____

_____

_____

_____

_____

_____

_____

_____

_____

_____

On the next few pages, write about
your favorite family gatherings.
Who do you **love** to be around?

_____
_____
_____
_____
_____
_____
_____
_____
_____
_____
_____
_____
_____
_____
_____
_____
_____
_____
_____
_____
_____

_____

_____

_____

_____

_____

_____

_____

_____

_____

_____

_____

_____

_____

_____

_____

_____

_____

_____

_____

_____

_____

_____

10

Fill the page with this sentence:
An endless supply of positive energy
flows around me at all times.

Fill the page with this sentence:
I see the beauty that exists in every person, place, and thing.

_____

_____

_____

_____

_____

_____

_____

_____

_____

_____

_____

_____

Fill the page with this sentence:
I have what it takes to make
all of my dreams come true.

_____

_____

_____

_____

_____

_____

_____

_____

_____

_____

_____
_____
_____
_____
_____
_____
_____
_____
_____
_____

Fill the page with this sentence:
I celebrate life and beauty every day.

_____
_____
_____
_____
_____
_____
_____
_____
_____
_____
_____

_____

_____

_____

_____

_____

_____

_____

_____

_____

_____

_____

_____

_____

Fill the page with this sentence:
Life is here for me to experience. I'm ready!

_____

_____

_____

_____

_____

_____

_____

_____

_____

_____

_____

_____

_____

Imagine the **warmest, brightest, loudest** feeling of love that ever existed. See that it can heal all wounds in any event. It is stronger than pain and fear every time. Tap into this truth as you use the space below to describe your ideal situation for love.

I love the **people** around me because:

_____

_____

_____

_____

I love the **place** where I live because:

_____

_____

_____

_____

I love the place where I **work** because:

_____

_____

_____

_____

I love my **creative** ideas because:

_____
_____
_____

I love my **beautiful** body because:

_____
_____
_____

I love this **planet** Earth because:

_____
_____
_____

I love my **AMAZING** life because:

_____
_____
_____

Fill the page with this sentence:

I have a tremendous amount of wealth to offer the world.

23

What are you **grateful** for?
On the next few pages, write in detail about
the things that get you excited about life.

_____

_____

_____

_____

_____

_____

_____

_____

_____

_____

_____

_____

_____

_____

_____

_____

_____

_____

_____

_____

_____

_____

_____

_____

_____

_____

_____

_____

_____

_____

_____

_____

_____

_____

_____

_____

_____

_____

_____

_____

_____

_____

_____

_____

_____

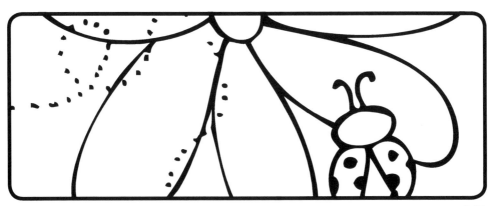

26

_____

_____

_____

_____

_____

_____

_____

_____

_____

_____

_____

_____

_____

Fill the page with this sentence:
My life is full of abundance and beauty.

_____

_____

_____

_____

_____

_____

_____

_____

_____

_____

_____

_____

_____

Create Your Own Mandala

A **Mandala** is a circular shape filled with repetitive, intricate patterns. The word is Sanskrit for **circle**. Psychologically, circles represent wholeness and unity. The shape is complete and of itself. It is **one**.

Let your mind **drift** while filling in each ring with pattern. **Observe** thoughts and feelings that flow through you. Allow things to pass. Let it all go.

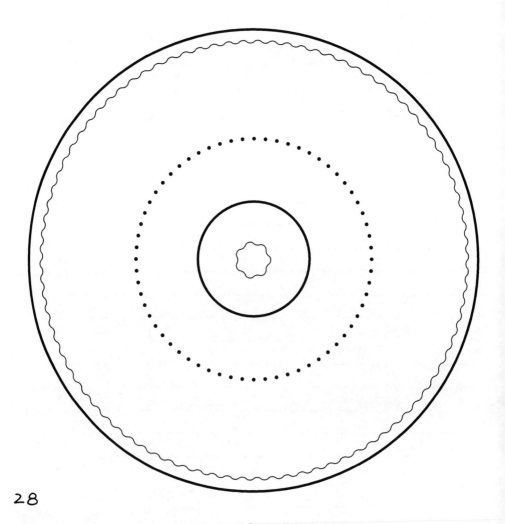

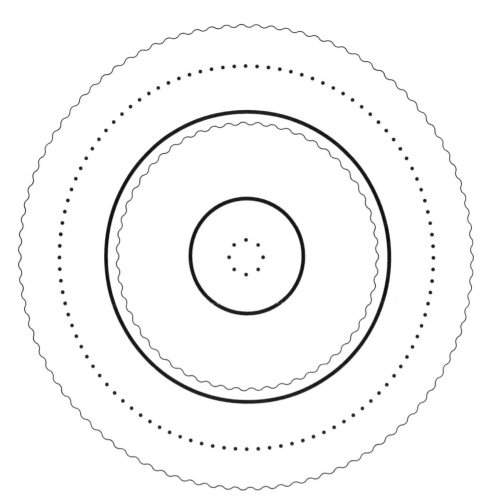

Now... Analyze Your Pattern Choices

Jagged, zigzag lines represent active energy and are best used when thinking about goals and dreams.

Squares and box shapes offer protection and are best used to strengthen stability, be it financial, emotional, physical, or spiritual.

Spirals and loops show progression and growth. Draw this pattern when interested in making changes.

Checkerboards, asterisks, or crisscross diamond designs depict a network of interactions. Use this design while visualizing strong relationships and infrastructures.

Fill the page with this sentence:
I have everything I need to be
happy, healthy, and whole.

31

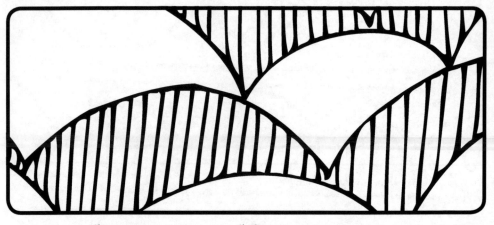

Do you **love yourself** as much as you should?

On the next couple of pages, **describe** in detail the things about yourself that make you different from everyone else.

Write about your personality; your quirks; your body type; your **style**; your **dreams**.

What makes you, **YOU**!?

_____
_____
_____
_____
_____
_____
_____
_____
_____
_____
_____
_____
_____
_____

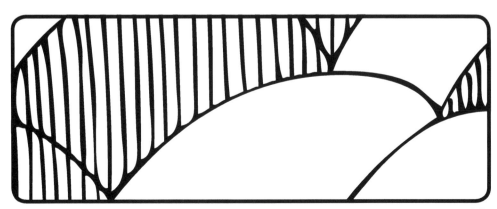

Fill the page with this sentence:
I enjoy my life's journey with anticipation and wonder.

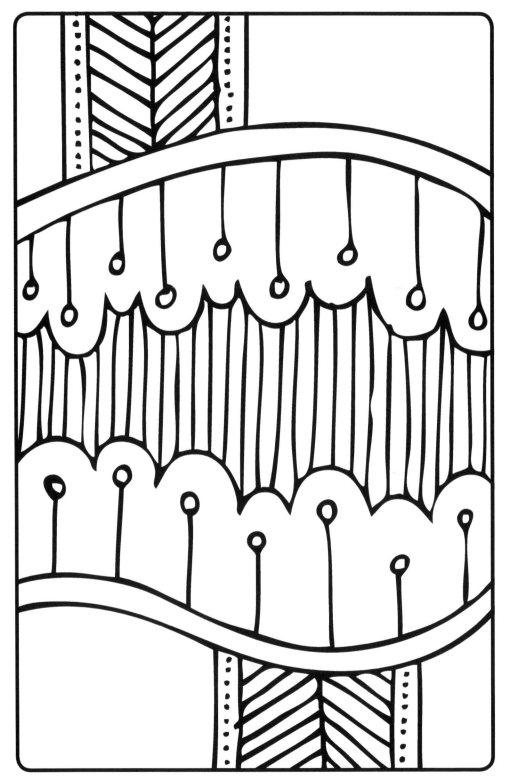

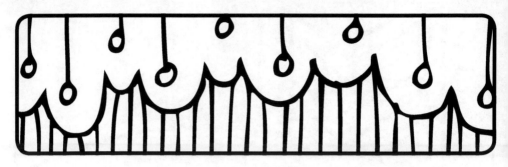

Put some headphones on and play your favorite **music**. Or, sit in a quiet room by yourself and listen to a song that makes you feel good.

Turn the lights down low, or close your eyes. On the next page, let your hand start **dancing** with the music as you draw and scribble lines and shapes.

If the music is slow and **romantic**, for example, you might find that your sketch is flowing and **carefree**. Loud, heavy metal music might inspire you to draw sharper, more rigid artwork.

Try this experiment several times with different types of music.

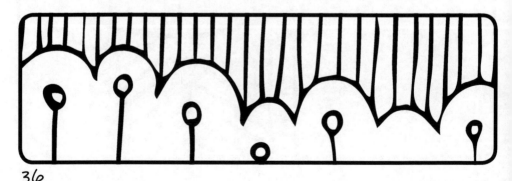

My world is filled with love,
happiness, and abundance.

I deserve to live a complete and full life.

I attract everything I need to be happy
by being myself.

Sometimes **doodling** is just the thing to do to quiet the mind. It's not always easy to get started.

On this page and the next are different shapes to encourage your **creativity**. Try drawing a picture using these objects.

If that doesn't appeal to you, simply start filling each area in with repetitive patterns. Use the sketches throughout this book to inspire your creativity.

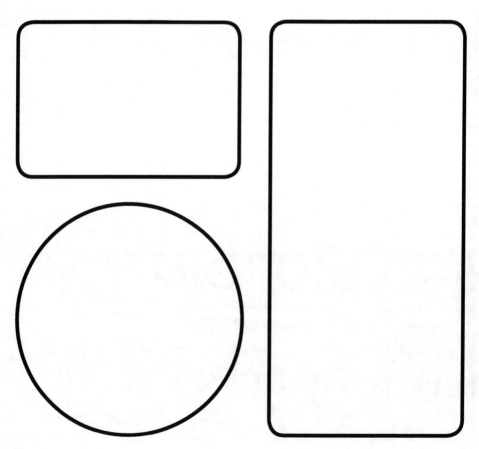

Try not to judge your **artwork**. Simply let it flow.
Let your mind wander into a land of **imagination**.

50

_____
_____
_____
_____
_____
_____
_____
_____
_____
_____
_____
_____
_____

Fill the page with this sentence:
I surround myself with people who love and support me.

_____
_____
_____
_____
_____
_____
_____
_____
_____
_____
_____
_____

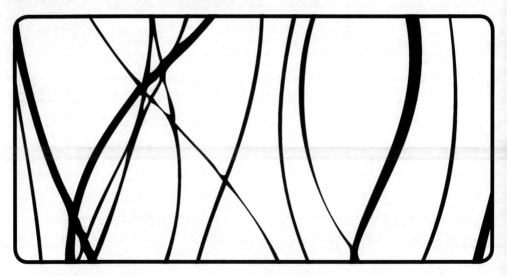

Imagine that you have your **dream job**. You find that the work itself is so rewarding you don't even notice the **million dollar paychecks** that are deposited regularly into your bank account.

On the next few pages, write about that job.
• Who do you work for?
• What type of job is it?
• What rewards are you receiving from your efforts?
• How does the world benefit from what you do?

_____

_____

_____

_____

_____

_____

_____

_____

_____

_____

_____

_____

_____

_____

_____

_____

_____

_____

_____

_____

_____

Fill the page with this sentence:
My love and zest for life inspires
and motivates people.

_____

_____

_____

_____

_____

_____

_____

_____

_____

_____

_____

Are you able to fully express your **appreciation** for the people who mean the most to you?

It's common to assume loved ones know our feelings. That is usually not true! Most people are unaware of our feelings until we've shared them with words or clear actions. Here's an exercise that can help you **communicate** your **gratitude** for loved ones.

Think of 5-15 people who you would want to take with you on a **dream vacation**. For each person, answer the following questions. Rewrite the answers into notes of gratitude. Call these people, or send them a letter explaining what it is that you appreciate about them.

You'll both feel better. **I promise.**

I love you because you're unique.
Here's how and why:

_____
_____
_____
_____

I felt loved and appreciated when you:

_____
_____
_____
_____
_____

I wanted you to know that you mean a
lot to me because:

_____
_____
_____
_____

Fill the page with this sentence:
I live a joyful, honest, and full life.

If you could be any **animal** in the world for just one day, what would you be and why?

_____
_____
_____
_____
_____
_____
_____
_____
_____
_____
_____
_____
_____
_____
_____
_____
_____
_____
_____

Fill the page with this sentence:
I create my dream life with enthusiasm.

63

What do you think is holding you back
from reaching your **dreams**?
Write whatever comes to mind here.

Then, in a day or two, come back with an open mind and
an open heart, and honestly ask yourself if what you wrote
is true or is it an excuse or limitation that can be removed.

_____

_____

_____

_____

_____

_____

_____

_____

_____

_____

_____

_____

_____

_____

_____

_____

_____

_____

_____

_____

_____

_____

_____

_____

_____

_____

_____

_____

_____

_____

_____

_____

_____

_____

_____

_____

_____

_____

_____

_____

Let's take a look at an **experience** from the past that feels heavy. Think of something that is affecting you today in a negative way. It can be a recent event or something from a long time ago.

It's time to let it go.

Visualize, imagine, and dream about the positive person that you want to become.

In the top box on the next page, draw a bold line through the words that reflect how this situation makes you feel.

In the second box, circle and/or highlight the words that describe how you want to feel from now on.

Draw or write about what each word means to you. Focus your energy on the words that you circled and **transform yourself** by focusing only on these positive feelings.

hurt   sad   lonely   scared   neglected
weak   ashamed   bullied   out-of-place
abused   ignored   deceived   betrayed
disturbed   unhealthy   depressed   bored
embarrassed   criticized   unclean
anxious   angry   bothered   troubled
scarred   hopeless   low   misunderstood

healed   happy   friendly
brave   proud   healthy
excited   honest   enthusiastic
peaceful   accepted   loving
hopeful   motivated   powerful
strong   blessed   faithful
accepting   forgiving   successful
prosporous   generous   wise
pleasant   calm   understood

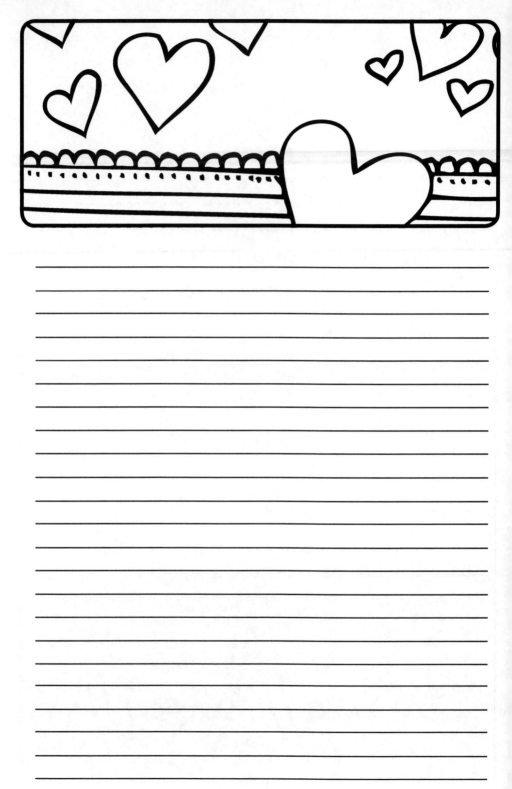

69

Fill the page with this sentence:
Miracles and magic surround me everywhere I go.

Describe your best friend's most **adorable** behaviors. Why do you think you're attracted to these **qualities**? Do you also have the same characteristics or are you complete opposites? What qualities do you think your **friends** find attractive about you?

_____
_____
_____
_____
_____
_____
_____
_____
_____
_____
_____
_____
_____
_____
_____
_____
_____

_____

_____

_____

_____

_____

_____

_____

_____

_____

_____

_____

_____

_____

_____

_____

_____

_____

_____

_____

_____

_____

74

Fill the page with this sentence:
I am open to receiving an abundance of
wealth, health, and happiness.

_____
_____
_____
_____
_____
_____
_____
_____
_____
_____
_____
_____
_____
_____
_____
_____
_____
_____
_____
_____
_____
_____

Start **doodling!**

Express your feelings creatively.

Think about the exercises you've completed in this book. Build **self-awareness** by answering the following questions:

- What have you discovered about yourself?
- What areas are you working on?
- What new exercises have you found to be helpful?
- What have you been able to let go of?

_____
_____
_____
_____
_____
_____
_____
_____
_____
_____
_____
_____
_____
_____
_____
_____

_____

_____

_____

_____

_____

_____

_____

_____

_____

_____

_____

_____

_____

_____

Fill the page with this phrase:

I share my gifts generously with others.
I accept others' gifts with gratitude.

_____

_____

_____

_____

_____

_____

_____

_____

_____

_____

_____

_____

Fill the page with this sentence:
People recognize and appreciate the love
that pours out of my being.

87

_____

_____

_____

_____

_____

_____

_____

_____

_____

_____

_____

Fill the page with this sentence:
I am open to experiencing
everything life has to offer.

_____

_____

_____

_____

_____

_____

_____

_____

_____

_____

_____

Go for a **quiet walk** today. Look for the items on this check list. Either take the book with you and check items off as you find them, or test your memory and see how many treasures you can remember when you get back home.

____ **squirrel**
____ **dog (not on a leash)**
____ **dog (on a leash)**
____ **cat in a window**
____ **three birds**
____ **fallen leaf**
____ **flower in bloom**
____ **a couple holding hands**
____ **someone smiling**
____ **a blue car**
____ **a red rock or stone**
____ **a bicycle**
____ **a motorcycle**
____ **standing water**
____ **a fire hydrant**
____ **a really beautiful tree**

____ a white house
____ children playing
____ a swing set
____ a bee, fly, or other insect
____ a shape in the clouds
____ something orange colored
____ a baby (human or animal)
____ the sun setting
____ the sound of laughter
____ something fuzzy
____ a stop sign
____ a pine tree
____ an alligator (hey, you never know)
____ a person in uniform
____ the sound of music
____ a piece of broken glass
____ the bud of a flower
____ an ant hole
____ a house with a green roof
____ a white fence
____ a funny yard decoration

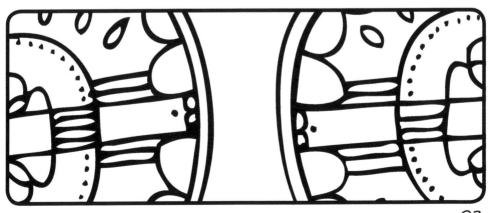

_____

_____

_____

_____

_____

_____

_____

_____

_____

_____

Fill the page with this sentence:
I create a wonderful life
by making positive choices.

_____

_____

_____

_____

_____

_____

_____

_____

_____

_____

95

98

Fill the page with this sentence:
I let go of the anger and pain in order to welcome new beginnings into my life.

Made in the USA
Middletown, DE
16 July 2015